Zen Seeds for Fallow Ground

Shoken

Shoken Winecoff

Ryumonji Zen Monastery

ISBN: 978-1-929919-67-3

Library of Congress Control Number: 2015951160

Camp Pope Publishing
PO Box 2232
Iowa City, Iowa 52244

www.camppope.com

Cover illustration by Carl Homstad.

All articles originally appeared in the Decorah Newspapers
and are reprinted here with permission.

Introduction

Zen seeds germinate when the ground is ready. These are teachings that are open to everyone.

If you've lived a little bit of life, you probably know what it means to have your ground tilled by life's plow. When the ground of your life has been turned over, you are ready receive these seeds.

These Zen seeds are teachings that I received from Dainin Katagiri, a Zen monk who came from Japan to the U.S. He founded the Minnesota Zen Meditation Center in Minneapolis during the 1970's. I began Zen meditation practice there when my own life-ground was being turned over. I was ready to receive the seeds of Zen practice and teachings.

Buddhist teachings are often shrouded in language that is not always easy to understand. The teachings in this book are for ordinary people. They originally appeared as articles in the Decorah, Iowa newspaper. They are human life stories. I hope they will speak to you. They are *Zen Seeds for Fallow Ground*.

Shoken Winecoff

Deep Appreciation

Dainin Katagiri

1928 – 1990

Dainin Katagiri Roshi was one of the early Soto Zen teachers who transmitted Zen Buddhism to the United States from Japan.

He provided the vision for building a monastery in the Midwest. Ryumonji Zen Monastery came from this vision. He transmitted his teaching to twelve Dharma heirs. I was the last person he ordained.

He left behind a legacy of recorded Dharma teachings which are available on the MZMC website.

Table of Contents

The Whole World is the Monastery

Oct. 30, 2006

Monasteries are not just for monks. There was an ancient Zen monk named Dogen who said "The whole world is the monastery."

I am a Zen monk. I live in a monastery, but I also live in the world. For me, I don't see a difference between living in the monastery and living in the world. In a sense, the whole world is our monastery.

We are called to be monks of the Universe. We are each born of the world and nurtured by the Universe. We are part of the earth and therefore should be stewards of the earth. A monk's life is to be a steward of the earth.

There was once a monk in the Buddha's time who took a vow to clean the earth. That's interesting! If you're bored and don't have purpose, how about taking a vow to clean the earth? It's your monastery.

Where do we live? I remember my dad fell and broke both wrists. He was living alone. So he went to a nursing home. He was not a "happy camper" in the nursing home. When I visited him he was depressed and had his chin in his oatmeal. I said, "Dad! Father Tom (the chaplain) needs an assistant. There's no way he can visit all these 'little old ladies.' (There were about a hundred women and five men in this retirement home, which belonged to an order of nuns.) You ought to start getting around and saying hello to people." Well, the next time I visited him he took me for a walk around the halls. He was beaming as he said hello to Matilda, to Myrtle, to Mary Lou, and he was also talking to the four other guys at his breakfast table. The retirement home had become his monastery. And everyone loved him.

It's easy to lose our purpose. We need to think bigger than just our small self. We are each other. You are the world. The world is you. To live there is to live "in" monastery.

A Flood of Devastation

September 6, 2007

In the summer of 2007 we had some terrible mud slides along the Mississippi River and a devastating flood just north of us. I saw first hand some of the results of these storms. The mud slides along the river bluffs took out everything in their path—trees, houses, you name it.
In Rushford, MN the devastation of the flood was everywhere. Huge dump trucks were picking up debris from the curb. The debris was the contents of people's homes. People were dragging everything they owned out onto the street. There were appliances, couches, carpeting, toys, TV's and on and on. I saw this mountain of "trash" piled two stories high stacked on what looked like a football field where trucks were piling up all the debris. You could see it from miles away. People lost everything they owned.

I felt saddened by the whole scene. When I looked into people's faces you could feel the devastation and bleakness that had set into their lives as they waded through the mud sorting through their belongings and trying to put their lives together.

I remembered the Buddha's teaching that
everything is impermanent. How do you
live when the heavens let go with a flood
of devastation or the earth shifts under
your feet? Impermanence is swift. It's hard
to hang onto self when you are swept away
by life's events.

Things go pretty well when everything is going
your way. But when things happen that are not
to our liking we can really get tossed. It takes
strength to stand up in muddy waters.
Forbearance does not come cheap. Sometimes a
deep breath is hard to find.

The great Zen Master Dogen once said, "Do not say
I arise, or I disappear. There is just arising and
disappearing." Sometimes we have to get ourselves
out of the way and just get on with what is!

The present moment is a "pivot of nothingness".
There's nothing to hang on to. Yet, how we handle
present moment interfaces with whole future.
The future is always right under our foot. It's why
ancient masters have said the essential thing is a matter
of everydayness. Real silence is not a matter of
searching for tranquil bliss. It's a practical matter of
standing up where things are! This is life's challenge!

Riding Along on a Trolley Bus

January 28, 2008

I had an unusual Christmas gift from my brother and his wife a few years ago. I was visiting them in St. Louis. My sister-in-law signed us up for one of those senior citizen outings. This was my first senior citizen outing! We went to see Christmas lights on a trolley bus. The trolley bus was all decked out with the usual holiday decorations and wooden bench seats and even a bell that clanged every time you pulled the cord.

We had a great time, singing Christmas carols, drinking hot chocolate, and viewing all the Christmas lights. However, on the way home it was late and we were about twenty miles outside the city limits. We were coming back into St. Louis on a six lane interstate highway. It was raining mixed with snow. Our little trolley bus was just chugging along at about 45 MPH, but the semi-trucks were coming up from behind us at 70 MPH.

We were sitting in the back seat of the trolley bus. As I looked back all I could see were these huge headlights roaring up behind us. It seemed like there was a sea of semi-trucks bearing down on us and then vearing into the lanes on either side of us just inches from our window. Most of the seniors seemed unaware of what was happening. Everyone was just singing along, drinking their hot chocolates, and having a great old time. But, outside there were thousands of pounds of steel hurtling past us at the speed of sound. We were in the vortex of the universe passing us by.

I thought to myself this is just the way life is: infinitely bigger than our awareness of what is and moving at a super-fast speed. Life is bigger than just you and me. As an ancient Zen master said, "You are not it. It is you." Think about that!

It's hard sometime to live with life as it is. We try to control everything. Our trolley bus is just one little speck of the reality of the Universe. Life includes the trolley, but it's also beyond. Speeding semis are also part of the reality.

Act with awareness. This requires a flexibile and magnanimous mind. If you're attached too much to your own way, you're heading for a collision. Life has its own rhythm. Old age, sickness, and death come up behind everyone. It is the express highway that we are all on. Wake up to the true moment!

Receiving What's Offered

June 26, 2008

A couple of months ago I started doing takuhatsu (mendicant begging) in nearby Decorah, Iowa. I was doing it there once a month, standing on a corner in full monk's robes with straw hat and begging bowl. In ancient times this is the way monks supported themselves.

It is also a symbol—for myself and for others—to just receive what's offered. It doesn't mean we shouldn't strive for things, or use all the means at our disposal to change the things that need to be changed in this world. But, in the final analysis, you have to be willing to just receive what's offered. Otherwise, you drive yourself crazy.

Recently I flew to Minneapolis. Usually I take the new light rail system into the city and then a local bus to where I'm staying. This last time it was getting pretty late, but I still took the public transportation. The bus was just about full. I sat down in the first empty seat that I came to. It was next to a man about my age in his late sixties.

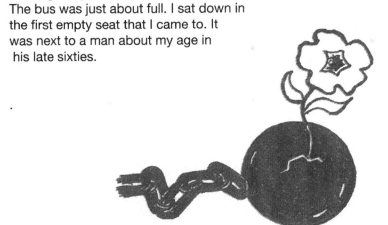

etsudo

He told me he had just recently been released from prison for a crime that he did not commit. He had been in prison for ten years! He appealed his case many times, but to no avail. Finally, someone confessed to the crime for which he was unjustly accused. There was something very peaceful about this man. He didn't talk bitterly. He was just happy to be alive and be able to do the things he had dreamed of while he was on the inside. He had learned to just receive what's offered. It's a tough lesson.

I told this story in one of our recent newsletters. The other day I received a letter from someone I know who was visiting a prisoner on death row. This is what she had to say: "What causes me to write now is your encounter with the man on the bus. I visit a man on death row—for something he didn't do. He knows more about patience than I'll probably ever learn. Yet it's my job to minister to him. You can probably guess who's learning the most here!"

You can't always control everything in your life. Life includes both favorable and unfavorable circumstances. You have to learn to deal with both.

You don't know true silence until you are boxed in a corner and can't move an inch. In that place you just receive what's offered. When you can do that you can move forward. This is true in many circumstances. It's true especially in older age, sickness, and even death.

So life teaches us about quietude, just receiving what's offered and coming back to what is. To stand up in quietude is empowering. It allows you to change the present and create the future.

Progress is Neither Far nor Near

November 13, 2008

"If I take one step forward, enlightenment unfolds. If backward, universal mind still appears. Even if I take no step forward or backward, I hope you will not say that my life is of no purpose." This is an ancient Zen saying.

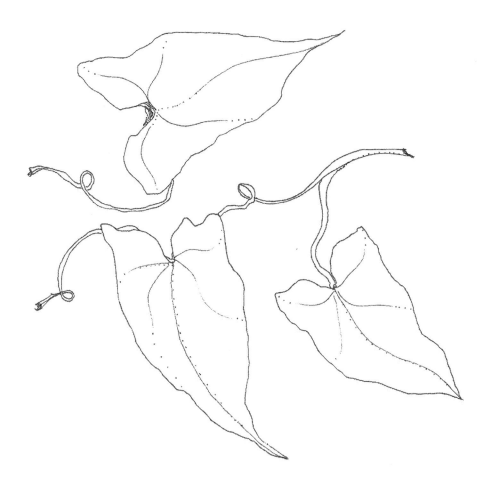

These three simple sentences encourage us to think about what constitutes real progress. What we think of as progress may not always actually be progress. Some of the ways of thinking and existing that we have considered to be progress in our modern civilization are now turning around to bite us. And what we think of as failure may not always necessarily be failure. Great learning can occur even when we feel that we have failed miserably. And just because there appears to be no movement, it doesn't mean everything is standing still. Things beyond our perception are still moving. That's why ancient Zen monk Sekito Kisen says, "Progress is not a matter of far nor near."

These are interesting thoughts to ponder as our country is occupied with elections and ideas of winning and losing, when the world is falling into economic recession, while oil supplies dwindle and earth temperatures rise. In the midst of winning and losing, rising and falling, we should try to keep in mind concepts of "no-winning," "no-losing," "no-rising," and "no-falling." Oil resources may dwindle, but this gives rise to alternative sources of energy that will greatly benefit the planet and its inhabitants.

When a leaf falls, there is a front side and a back side. Often we see just the side that faces up. The other side is there even though it is hidden. Just because you "win", it doesn't necessarily mean you win. There's a lot to lose in winning. And just because you "lose", it doesn't necessarily mean you lose. You can learn valuable lessons in losing.

We thought we were winning when the stock market was so high, and investments soaring, and gas so cheap. But now people are stuffing money in their mattresses, and raising chickens, and thinking twice about big investments. Maybe this is not such a bad thing.

We all have our ideas about "progress". We usually swim on the surface of the ocean, but actually we should be walking on the bottom of the ocean. This is the vast dimension where everything is interpenetrated with everything else. Don't get tossed by the surface of the waves. Just walk in the vast Ocean where progress is neither far nor near.

We've Forgotten How to Walk

March 26, 2009

The other day I was driving up to the Twin Cities from Decorah. I was getting a little drowsy when I saw a hitch-hiker walking on the side of the road. I pulled over and picked him up. He was walking on Highway 52 from Fountain, MN to Rochester, MN. That's over 25 miles!

The man told me his car had been impounded from his workplace parking lot and he didn't have money to get it out. He had been making the walk for several days to Rochester where he had a job. He said he got a few rides, but most of the time he walked the whole way.

Twenty-five miles is a long way to walk. But this man was at ease with it and didn't complain. During our conversation he said to me, "We've forgotten how to walk."

That's true about a lot of things. We get used to having things in a certain way. We think that's the way they've always been and always will be. Take the economy, for example. With the bottom falling out, we are forced to think differently and it changes our perspective. We've all had to think more about where we are now and what we really need.

We like having things according to our own convenience. But life has its own twists and turns; it is constantly changing and adjusting. There is old age, sickness, and death. We have to remember how to walk in all the situations of life.

We can have our own ideas about things, but ideas can be just another source of human suffering. We have to move beyond our ideas and learn how to be in harmony with heaven and earth. Otherwise we suffer from the delusion that the world revolves around us, rather than the truth that we revolve around the world. The more we hold on to our ideas, the more we suffer.

The Buddha said, "If you want to shed afflictions, you should observe contentment. The state of contentment is the abode of prosperity and happiness, peace and tranquility. Those who are content may sleep on the ground and still consider it comfortable; those who are not content would be dissatisfied even in heaven. Those who are not content are always caught up in sensual desires; they are pitied by those who are content."

To be content is to take a breath and take inventory of where things are. It's to turn your light inward and reflect on where things are now. It's recognizing what's what and walking from there.

I learned a lot from the young hitch-hiker. I thought of the ages when Native American women and men walked great distances. We too should remember how to walk the distances that present themselves now.

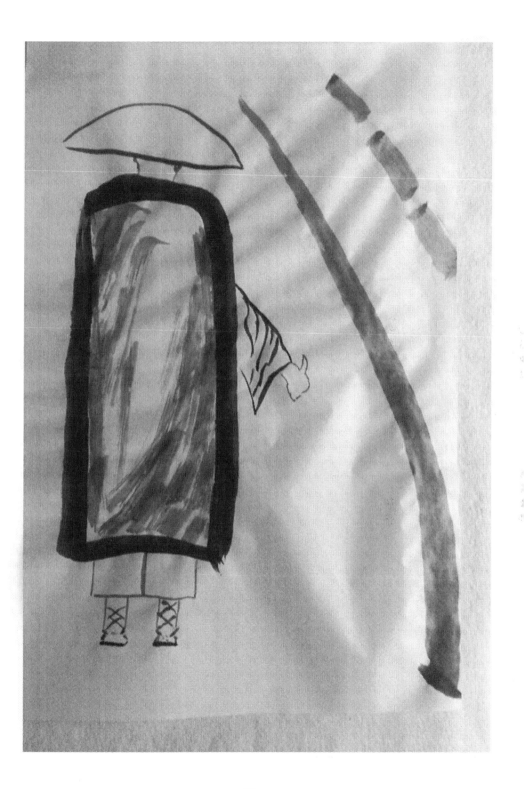

Facing the Wall

July 7, 2009

Everyone faces a wall at times. The wall is your life. It's right in front of you. I get up every morning and sit in a meditation hall facing the wall. My day is right there. I don't know exactly what the day will bring. I may have an idea of what the day will be like, but there's no guarantee what will transpire. My part is to wholeheartedly face the day whatever it brings.

To face the day is to drop off body and mind. Facing the day means you might have to drop off what you feel or think. You might have ideas of how things should be, but to embrace the day means to bring yourself to the day as it is. If you tend to be tossed by things easily, it can be difficult to get through a day.

I studied for twenty years with a Zen monk, Rev. Dainin Katagiri. His life was just going like a river. Things didn't always go his way, but his life was just going. He wasn't so tossed by things. I respected his steady way of living. I appreciated his zazen practice of sitting facing the wall. It helped me with the walls I was facing in my own life.

True living involves learning how to live even when we are driven into a corner and can't move an inch. This feeling of hopelessness is indeed facing the wall.

The great matter that we all face is life and death. We face it in ourselves and with our family and friends. Impermanence is swift; we can't always be prepared for everything.   A gasp is part of everyone's life! I have a friend who is a hospice worker. A while back he was attending a dying woman. Her two sons sat with their mother for hours. At the moment their mother took her final breath, the one son let out a gasp. The great matter is a bolt of lightning in the night.

I heard a talk recently by the Dalai Lama. Looking out over a crowded convention center he said, "One thing's for sure. In a hundred years we'll all be dead!" There was a stone silence in the convention center. The Dalai Lama just smiled. And then a warm glow came up in everyone. Death is a wall we all must face.

Everyone hates to see petals fall and weeds grow. The nature of life is that it is constantly changing. Gray clouds eventually pass and harsh winds cease.

This is my sitting every morning quietly facing the wall.

The Last, the Lost, and the Least

November 23, 2009

I was recently in northern Minnesota. I know an elderly couple up there whose son is a church pastor. They told me a story of one of his parishioners who was recently murdered. They said the parishioner was a gentle man who cared for the last, the lost, and the least that he met on the streets and in the woods of northern Minnesota. Unfortunately, he was killed by one of these people.

The pastor of this church has a ministry devoted to the poor and indigent peoples of northern Minnesota. He did not want this terrible death to deter others from reaching out to vulnerable people. In a letter to his parishioners he said, "We cannot excuse murder by simply claiming alcoholism and mental illness as a defense. Murder under any circumstances is a profound transgression against the fifth commandment and must be dealt with accordingly. But we must never let our fears of the rare times when something goes bad keep us from reaching out to the homeless, especially our mentally ill, chemically dependent, and intellectually disabled folks."

I was touched by the pastor's commitment to serve the last, the lost, and the least. We often let fear and indifference overwhelm us in our response to difficult situations. I think this is also true of how we relate to people whose cultural backgrounds are different from our own. I was especially moved by this pastor's willingness to reach out to all people even if they look, think, or act differently.

All religions have compassion at the heart of their teachings. True compassion is based on wisdom. The wisdom we are talking about is to see the inter-dynamic nature of all existence. Compassion flows from seeing our common existence even if people seem different from us.

The trouble is we like to pick and choose when and where we exercise our compassion. There are always the last, the lost, and the least individuals that challenge the depth and breadth of our compassion. They are not really so different from us. Wisdom and compassion help us to appreciate the oneness that binds us together in the human family. Religious practice must include the whole world.

The Land That's Neither Hot nor Cold

July 22, 2010

On a hot summer day we complain about the heat and dream of some cool place up north. On a cold winter day we dream of a warm tropical island someplace. But where is the place that's neither hot nor cold?

There's a Zen koan that addresses this question: A monk asks, "Where is the land that's neither hot nor cold?" Another monk responds, "When it's hot be with hotness and when it's cold be with coldness!"

I thought the land that's neither hot nor cold was Hawaii, or someplace with good air conditioning and heating. But . . . the true land that's neither hot nor cold is the mind space of where you are. Be one with hotness when it's hot, and be one with coldness when it's cold. That's it! No discussion. Take care of where you are!

Taking care of where you are is like putting a strainer in a stream. You can't lift water out of the stream with a strainer. The way to get out of coldness is to be one with the coldness and the way out of the heat is to be one with the hotness. As you soak in hotness, there's no "hot" even though your shirt is wet with sweat. When it's hot it's hot!

K SWEET

The other day my brother and his son where working on building a chicken coop. This was in St. Louis where the temperatures were up in the 100's. His son was complaining about the heat, but my brother just kept moving. Together they finished the chicken coop.

A Zen master said, "If the least like or dislike arises, the mind is lost in confusion." In other words, we can really be tossed around by our likes and dislikes. When there's a big gap between "what is" and "your response to what is," there's suffering. Suffering depends on how you respond to any given situation. No one likes it when it's too hot but your response to hotness can be a greater source of suffering than the hotness itself.

You can get pretty bummed out by circumstances. We always want to control our own "thermostat". But sometimes the only release is to embrace the situation you are in.

So where is this land that's neither hot nor cold? It's right under your foot. Take care of where you are. It's the ultimate vacation land that's neither hot nor cold.

War Torn

Nov. 18, 2010

A few weeks ago, on one of those "thought-for-the-day" calendars, I read a commentary on war by the Tibetan monk, the Dalai Lama. This is what he had to say:

"We should think carefully about the reality of war. Most of us have been conditioned to regard military combat as exciting and glamorous—an opportunity for men (and women) to prove their competence and courage. Since armies are legal, we feel that war is acceptable; in general, nobody feels that war is criminal or that accepting it is a criminal attitude. In fact, we have been brainwashed. War is neither glamorous nor attractive. It is monstrous. Its very nature is one of tragedy and suffering."

War is far from most of us unless you, a family member, or a close friend is serving in the military. But if you're close to it, you may have tasted the truth of what the Dalai Lama is saying.

A few weeks ago I was in Japan and had occasion to visit the city of Hiroshima. We visited the Peace Park and stood where in 1945 an atomic bomb exploded 600 meters overhead. With one pull of the trigger over 200,000 people were killed. The day we visited the bombsite a hundred Japanese children were gathered there singing songs of peace. They were offering origami "peace" cranes in memory of the scores of children who were vaporized in that atomic blast. I was touched by the tender beauty and innocence of their voices.
I thought of the thousands of similar innocent children's voices that were lost in one atomic blast.

When we were leaving the park an elderly Japanese gentleman asked me how we felt when we came to this Peace Park. I could not make a response. He read the sadness in my eyes.

War is not glamorous. It is not attractive. We should strive for more enlightened ways.

Potholes

March 17, 2011

Someone asked me, "What is the essence of life?" I answered, "Potholes."

Potholes are like the holes in the road that we try to avoid. But, it's inevitable that we sometimes hit them. It's easy to live happily when everything's going your way. But potholes are part of life. And sometimes we hit them. They can't always be avoided. How we handle the potholes in life is the essence of living.

Potholes can be our teachers. When you hit a few potholes in your life, you can begin to slow down and take notice. Even the really deep potholes can open you up to a different dimension of your life.

It is said, "When you're boxed in a corner and can't move an inch, this is where life begins." This is the point when you realize you don't have control over everything. It's the point where you have to stand up with things as they are.

We never know when or where we will encounter potholes. Life has its own spin. Even with our best efforts to control things, the universe has its own movement. You and I are not necessarily at the center of it.

Being a teenager has its potholes. Being married has its potholes. The bigger potholes are old age, sickness and death. Life goes pretty fast, but the game's not over until it's over.

Life is pretty precious. Potholes are just temporary junctures. In the big picture of things a pothole is just a sliver of time. Use this precious life. Do something positive. A smile, a hug, or just stooping down to listen to someone is a great gift . . . both for giver and receiver.

Living life is not always easy. Sometime days are gray. But grey clouds pass! And sometimes winters seem to never end. But spring is in the heart of winter.

The other day I saw workers filling potholes. Spring must be on its way. I hope all your roads will be "smooth".

Rocks
from Heaven

July 21, 2011

You never know what a day will bring. For instance, it's not every day that rocks fall from the sky. The other day was such a day!

Crews were rebuilding our county road. It had been a long-time plan to pave this section of gravel road that passes by our monastery. They were about to blast away a huge part of the bluff in order to straighten out the roadway. We had been forewarned that there would be some blasting that day. Safety precautions were all carefully in place.

Early that morning I saw one of the workers in our back yard with a seismograph. He was getting ready to measure the intensity of the blast that was about to take place down in the valley. I stepped out onto the back porch and shouted down to him, "Are you getting ready to blast?" He replied, "Yeah, in a few seconds."

With that, the blast went off! I heard the thundering crack . . . and then saw a rock shooting up into the sky! It traveled quite a distance upward. And then I heard rocks from heaven falling all around us. The worker dove behind a nearby tree and I pressed myself up against the wall of our building underneath the roof eave to protect my head.

I could hear the rocks falling all around. They were coming from so high in the sky that I couldn't even see them as they came down. I heard one of the rocks hit the roof of one of our buildings. I didn't know which building it hit, but later in the afternoon when I was putting away the tractor I saw a big hole in the roof of the barn and a shattered window where the rock clipped it as it came through the roof. Wow! I couldn't believe it, but there it was--the rock lying on the floor of the barn.

Fortunately, nobody was injured. The barn roof and window were promptly repaired. That night as I went to bed I thought, "You never know what a day will bring!"

This is a basic teaching. To live your life you have to be alive in whatever the day brings. Life! Death! Even rocks from heaven!

There's a little morning prayer that says:

> "Waking up this morning I vow with all beings,
> to realize everything without exception,
> embracing the ten directions."

To "realize everything" means to deal with whatever is in front of you. "Embracing the ten directions" means be prepared for whatever comes, whether it's from the north, south, east, west, northeast, northwest, southeast, southwest, up or down. In other words, avoid "picking and choosing" mind. Embrace the day as it is! Sunny day is sunny day. Gray day is gray day. Some days rocks fall from heaven!

The Dragon's Pearl

November 24, 2011

Once upon a time there was a friendly little dragon named Gulliver. Gulliver lived in the deep ocean. He spent most of his time playing around the surface. You could see him splash up and down once in a while if you were watching for him. Some people thought he was rather mysterious.

One day he encountered an old man in a fishing boat. The old man was not afraid of Gulliver, even though Gulliver had a ferocious looking face and a breath of fire that would knock your socks off. On that day, the old man in the fishing boat told Gulliver that there was a precious pearl at the bottom of the ocean. Gulliver had never gone down that far into the ocean before. So Gulliver decided that he would dive down and venture deep to look for the precious pearl.

When he got to the bottom of the ocean it was dark down there. But he found that there were hundreds and thousands of pearls all over the ocean floor. So Gulliver with a swoosh and a swirl scooped up in his jaws one of the precious pearls and came back up to the surface. He found the old man in the fishing boat again and said, "I thought you told me there was one precious pearl, but there are myriad pearls everywhere." Then the old man said, "Yes... every moment is a precious pearl! And there are hundreds and thousands of moments in one precious life-time!"

Gulliver scratched his head and let out a sigh, "Every moment is a precious pearl? What does that mean?" The old man said, "Well, every moment contains all the moments of the past, and influences all the moments of the future!" So Gulliver had a light bulb go off in his head and said, "Oh, I get it! Every moment is very precious!" And the old man said, "Yes, and we should handle each moment with utmost care like taking care of a precious jewel, even the moments we don't particularly like."

Then Gulliver said, "Well, what about when the ocean gets scary and big waves rise up and crash down?" The old man said, "Well, even these too can be precious moments. The ocean, you know, is not always smooth. Sometimes there are big waves. But when a little dragon passes through these waves, a little dragon can grow in strength. This is called the dragon gate where little dragons become great dragons. So even when you encounter big waves, it can be a precious pearl."

Gulliver looked deeply into the eyes of the old man. His face looked wrinkly and his eyes looked tired. Gulliver said, "You are an old man. You will die soon. How can this be a precious moment?" The old man smiled and said, "Yes, but even when we die it is truly a precious moment for those who come after us. When others see that we are gone they may be sad, but they will rise up and take our place and this will be a great treasure for many beings."

Gulliver swam home that night. When he climbed into bed he thought how fortunate he was to meet the old man. Gulliver knew that every moment is a precious pearl, even the moments that sometimes crash down on you. He learned to appreciate each day-- even the days that are grey and stormy. Gulliver learned to live with the sea and go with the waves. Then Gulliver let out a big yawn, pulled the covers up around his ears, and fell sound asleep.

Muddy Roads

March 22, 2012

The other day when I was coming back from Minneapolis
I turned up the road to our monastery and saw a big truck
loaded with gravel trying to get up our steep hill. This is a hill
that has defeated many a car and truck in winter ice and snow.
Anyway, the truck was grinding away, slipping and sliding
deeper and deeper into the soft spring mud that was oozing out
of the road. Eventually the truck was stuck in ruts so deep that
you could almost walk through them up to your knees.
The driver and I both stood there scratching our heads.
These are the precious moments!

Muddy roads are the stuff of life. Everyday life has its muddy roads. It's easy to get bogged down by things. Everyone wants to cruise along on a smooth, clear highway. How you handle the mud in your life is the virtue of living.

I trudged up the hill to the barn. My shoes were so packed with mud that they weighed a ton. I pulled out our old tractor. This is a small tractor and the truck was really big. But this is where we were! We hooked up the chains, and finally managed to pull the truck out of the ruts to the top of the hill. I felt like the little engine that could!

There's a Zen saying, "The lotus blooms in muddy water." It's really true! The beautiful lotus blooms from the nutrients in muddy water. We don't have to go around looking for mud. Everyday life has its share. It doesn't take much to get bogged down in it, but that's where the lotus blooms. Sometimes things work out and go smoothly. But sometimes they don't. Being stuck is not always the end of the world. We grow in moments of "stuckness."

Muddy roads come in many forms. Our challenge in life is to stand up in whatever circumstances we encounter. It won't be long and we'll probably be talking about summer drought instead of spring mud. Whatever season you find yourself bogged down in, just be one with whatever it is. Then you can say, "Spring, Summer, Fall, Winter. All beautiful!"

When the Well Runs Dry

August 2, 2012

This summer has been a time of extreme drought. People have been feeling it all across the country. We got a little rain recently, but things are still pretty parched. We discovered a few weeks ago that our well was running dry!

We take a lot for granted when it comes to water. When you turn on a faucet, you just expect water to come. When I first came to this area, we were thinking of building a Zen practice center on some country land in southeast Minnesota near New Albin, Iowa. At that time there was no well on the land so we had to carry water from a nearby spring. We valued that water. We carried it up bucket by bucket. It was just what we had to do. Later, we pumped water from that spring to an elevated tank outside a temporary kitchen building. We really thought it was a luxury to have "running" water.

The practice center on this land was closed after the death of its founder Katagiri Roshi. At that time I came to Decorah, Iowa. Eventually we acquired some land near Decorah, and that's how we began Ryumonji Zen Monastery. This was in the year 2000. At that time there was nothing on the land but a broken-down farm house with snakes in the walls and racoons in the basement. There was an old well with a broken pump handle and a cistern that gravity-fed the farm house. It was not a very deep well. It eventually ran dry.

So what do you do when the well runs dry? There are no guarantees that the wells in your life will continually produce water. Wells dry up. We take a lot for granted.

Katagiri Roshi's intention for building the country Zen practice center was: "I wish to build a place and an environment to practice the Way revering the ancient ways. Modern life is artificially protected. When the artificial environment collapses, for instance in a natural disaster or an economic calamity, people suffer severely. Modern people, therefore, need to live in direct contact with nature and find a practice method in tune with nature's rhythm. I am convinced we must build such a practice place in America."

Nature has its own rhythm. You can't always control everything. If you try to scoop up water with a strainer, you're not going to get very much. You'd do better to put the strainer in the water. You stand up where you are. This is liberation!

Home for Thanksgiving

December 13, 2012

I went home for Thanksgiving where my brother lives. They do a great family dinner every year. My brother cooks the turkey. This year everything was ready, except there was no cream for the coffee.

It was still early morning. My brother and I hopped into his pickup truck to go to their local gas station to pick up the cream. On the way, we spotted a big chocolate labrador running loose on the street. My brother said it looked like one of the neighbor's dogs, so we tried to catch him. The dog ran across a busy street and into the gas station. We caught him there. He was a strong dog, lunging back and forth, and difficult to hold. I held him while my brother got a leash out of the back of his pickup truck. Finally, we got him into the truck. But it turned out he wasn't the neighbor's dog. So we brought him home.

We broke the news to my sister-in-law that we had another "guest" for Thanksgiving dinner. She just about croaked when she saw the size of this labrador! We named him Big Max. My brother and his wife still had a kennel in their backyard for their own lab which had died the year before. We put Big Max in the kennel. He drank almost a whole bucket of water.

After a while, my brother wanted to take the dog for a walk. When we got to the nature trail, Big Max leaped out of the back of the pickup truck with my brother hanging on to the other end of the leash. My brother kept hollering, "Heel! Heel!" But within seconds Big Max had my brother hog-tied at the ankles and dragged him over a low-slung nature trail sign. My brother is a big guy, but Big Max slammed him down so hard that he bruised just about every rib in his rib cage. On top of that, Big Max had to relieve himself so badly from all that water he drank that he urinated on a tree within inches of my brother's head. I was impressed with my brother's even-tempered reaction despite the shock of it all.

You never know what life can bring you! We tried to find the rightful owners, but no luck. That evening Big Max was howling in the kennel. He wanted to get out and go home. The next morning we saw that Big Max had leaped over the five-foot-tall kennel fence. He had jumped up on an old over-turned flower pot. Over the fence he flew. Gone home for the holidays, wherever that might be!

So where is home? Home is right under your foot wherever you might be! Take a deep breath – drop off body and mind – and merge with situations as they are. You are home free! Still, you might want to keep an eye out for an old flower pot.

Happy Holidays

Spring Rains

April 25, 2013

When it rains it is said that "the phoenix is happy". The rains soak the earth. Green things start to sprout. People are relieved to feel the sweet drops on their tongues. But spring rains can also bring floods and turmoil for people. Sometimes cold and wet weather hangs on in the spring and you can't get out to start working in your garden and fields. Why is the world not cooperating for me to do all those spring things that I want to be doing? We say this is the time to be out there.

And then there's summer. It's warm, it's pleasant, and the garden grows. But it also can be hot and dry, and we struggle to stay cool, and we pray for rain. We hope for no drought, no tornadoes, or any other disasters, but there are no guarantees. It's hard at times to receive what the universe offers.

Sometimes we say life isn't fair. But who's to say what's fair? Everything has its own rhythm. We want things to go according to our idea. But the turnings of universe have their own spin.

Learning to be one with what is takes a great human spirit. It takes humility. It takes courage. And it takes faith. Faith is more than believing. Faith is to continue. It is said, "If you can maintain continuity, you are truly host within the host."

It's like a dragon gaining the water and a tiger entering the mountain. Dragons and tigers are great creatures. Their greatness is that they embrace wholeheartedly what is. They become one with water and mountain. This requires strength and courage.

Life has its sobering moments. Who said it would be easy? I don't have the answers. I get stumped like everyone else. But if you take a breath and stand up -- this is the Way of the ancients and holy ones. This is where fish become dragons and kitty cats become tigers.

There's more to face than just spring rains. We're all dealing with the larger issues of life and death. Each season is what it is. And so too with life and death.

We are all just a small breath in the life of universe.

Four Ducks on a Pond

September 12, 2013

You never know what might show up in your life. The other day four ducks showed up in our monastery pond. They were big white domestic ducks. A neighbor thought they were just the thing we needed at the monastery. They're very cute ducks . . . "quack, quacking" . . . and splashing all around.

They also are very large and juicy. And we have heard some coyotes and seen some big raccoons that are hanging around here. So everyone said we should build a duck house to protect the ducks from the critters. One thing leads to another. The ducks needed a duck house. So we built a duck house.

The duck house started out as a simple project, but ended up as an elaborate mansion. It's complete with insulation, electric lights, sliding doors, windows and more. I started thinking this wouldn't be a bad place for me to retire some day!

Life is constantly moving. Things change and sometime it's beyond your own idea. I had no idea of getting four ducks for the monastery. But everyone enjoys the ducks and they bring a nice dimension to monastery life.

When life brings you more than you expect, can you hang on to your seat? Sometimes it's more than you think you can handle. It's hard to be with things as they are! This is true in life and in death. It's also true of living with four ducks.

Four ducks are an opportunity to stretch your mind. It's what we call magnanimous mind. Magnanimous mind is neither biased nor contentious. It's beyond liking or disliking. It's a way of being with what is. You may not think ducks are any fun, but you'll never know until you get to know one.

Actually I like the four ducks in the pond. But in a few years we could have twenty ducks. Two are male and two are female.

Sometimes there's nothing to say. Just "Naka naka". It's a Japanese phrase. "What can you say?" The four ducks have there own word. "Quack Quack".

May your life go well.

Living by Vow

Living by vow is the vow to live! To live is not always easy.
Most of us do pretty good when things are going our way,
but when things are not going our way it can get pretty difficult.

The other day I went up to our barn to feed our ducks.
When I got there I discovered one of the four ducks was
no longer there. There was just a pile of feathers. Somebody
had had a tasty meal. I was sad to see we had lost one of
our ducks. Sometimes life just doesn't go as we want it to.
The universe has its own rhythms. Even with our best efforts
life doesn't always go our way.

So how do you live life as it is? It requires living by vow. It's
different from living by habit. Living by habit is linked to having
your desires fulfilled. If our desires are fulfilled we are usually
pretty happy. But when our desires are not fulfilled, we can
get pretty disheartened. Sometimes we even want to give
up on living. Habit is reinforced by reward. If there's no reward,
we don't want to continue.

On the other hand, living by vow is taking care of life as it is.
It's beyond "reward" or "no-reward". For example, people
may not pat you on the head even if you're a good person.
Reward is not always forthcoming. But you do the right thing
because it's the right the thing to do.

I say a morning "prayer" when I swing my feet off the bed:

> "Waking up this morning, I vow with all beings to realize
>   everything without exception, embracing the ten directions."

It's a good way to start the day. You never know what the
day will bring. So start with vowing to take care of whatever
the day brings you. This is to realize everything. Embracing
the ten directions means putting your arms around whatever comes.

Living by vow starts with attending to the little things in your life.
When it's time to get up, get up. When it's time to eat your breakfast,
eat your breakfast. When it's time to wash your dishes, wash
your dishes.

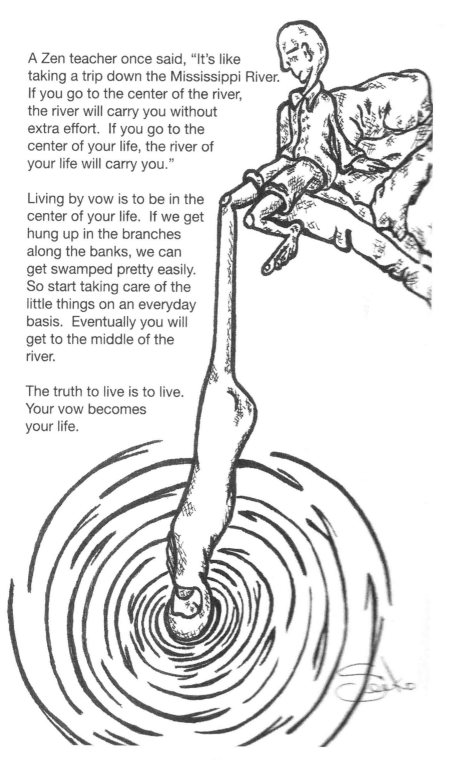

A Zen teacher once said, "It's like taking a trip down the Mississippi River. If you go to the center of the river, the river will carry you without extra effort. If you go to the center of your life, the river of your life will carry you."

Living by vow is to be in the center of your life. If we get hung up in the branches along the banks, we can get swamped pretty easily. So start taking care of the little things on an everyday basis. Eventually you will get to the middle of the river.

The truth to live is to live. Your vow becomes your life.

Hitting the Mark

There was once a young Japanese boy of 14 who was drafted into the Japanese military. His training was to become a kamikaze pilot. The first lessons in the training had to do with learning how to pilot a glider. Ten Japanese boys would pull a glider as fast as they could run. One boy would run behind the glider with a tow rope to keep the glider from flying off. The instructor would shout to the young pilot, "Keep your eye on the mark!" The mark was a pine tree at the end of the field.

When the young trainee pilot was proficient enough, they would let go of the rope and the glider would take off into the air. When this young boy that I'm talking about took off and became airborne, he lost sight of his mark and couldn't see the pine tree. He pulled the glider up too high, and then he pushed the controls down too far. . . and crash! The glider crashed into the ground. They pulled him out of the wrecked glider and that was the end of his career as a kamikaze pilot.

This young boy was Dainin Katagiri. At age 18, Katagiri became a monk, and eventually came to the United States and introduced Zen Buddhism to the Upper Midwest of North America. I'm glad Katagiri Roshi flunked the test of becoming a kamakazi pilot!

I heard him tell this story at the Minnesota Zen Meditation Center in Minneapolis. His teaching was that it is very important to keep your eye on the mark! And what is the mark? The mark is to be on target with life as it is. Life is not always the way we want it to be. We have our ideas about how things should be and can become attached to those ideas. But the reality of the way things are may be a lot different from how we want them to be. The reality is the pine tree. To hit the mark is to see the reality of things just as they are and adjust ourselves to deal with them straight on.

Often we mistake our ideas of the mark for the mark itself. When things are going our way, we're happy. When things are not going our way, we get bent out of shape. Sometimes we pull our glider too high in the sky with our nose pointing up. Sometimes we push down too far and crash into the ground. The pine tree is still out there, but we've lost sight of it.

So hitting the mark means bringing your mind into harmony with what is. To hit the mark is to stand up in what is. It involves keeping your wing tips straight and level, and when a gust of wind throws you off balance, bringing yourself back to straight and level. It's daily life! If you can hit the mark on a daily basis, your life goes pretty smoothly. If you're off the mark, you end up a wreck. So keep your eye on the mark!

Pontoon Ride November 6, 2014

One of the highlights of my summer this year was a pontoon ride on the Mississippi River. When a friend of mine who owns a pontoon boat asked me if I wanted to take a ride on the river, I didn't hesitate. "Sure," I said. "Let's go!"

Well, a pontoon boat isn't much like a boat. It's actually a raft that rests on two big, long, floating tin cans. And the raft itself is heavy aluminum. It would probably sink like a rock without the pontoons supporting it. The Mississippi River is a big river for a couple of floating tin cans. If you've ever been close to it, you can get a feeling for how huge it is and how much water is moving.

On the pontoon, everything was going along fine until I noticed some pretty big trees floating half-submerged down the river. It wouldn't take much for one of those trees to knock a big hole in one of those pontoon tin cans.

It occurred to me that this is a lot like life. We don't realize how vulnerable we are out there on the river of life. We're supported by the river, and yet we are also at the mercy of the river. You can wear a life preserver, but still anything can happen.

Our usual way is to float along in blissful ignorance. We don't even realize that we're being carried along by a huge stream of life. There's a lot that's hidden below the surface. We don't see the whole picture. All we see is the present moment.

If a tree comes floating down the river and smashes into your pontoon boat, it's not personal. It's just the river of the universe following its course. It feels personal when these things happen to us. There can be a lot of genuine pain and suffering. But the universe is just working, as it does, beyond our intellectual speculation and understanding.

Anyway, we had a great ride! We weren't hit by any big logs. However, when we got off the pontoon boat and were walking back on the dock, I almost stepped right off the edge of the dock as it narrowed toward the end. I came close to ending up waist deep in Mississippi mud!

If you want to stay out of the mud, you must attend to every moment at hand, not just the ones on the pontoon boat. Take care of every moment that is under your foot. If you can do that, your life is just going. It is the life of the universe.

The Monk and the Farmer

I was on a return flight from a conference a while back when I sat down in a seat next to a person who was a farmer. He asked me what I did. I said, "I teach meditation." He replied, "Ugh, I don't believe in meditation. I'm a farmer! I don't have time to be just sitting around."

Then we just sat there . . . in silence. At first I thought we didn't have much in common. But then as we got talking I said, "Well, we both plow rows and pull weeds." And he said, "Really?" I said, "You plow rows and pull weeds to help seeds grow, and I plow rows and pull weeds to help minds grow. We both cultivate growth."

Also I reflected that we both deal in manure. For the farmer, manure is a fact of life. Manure is the stuff that makes things grow. The farmer puts back into the land what he takes out of the land. For me, I also deal in "manure". The manure in our mind sometimes makes us grow. Life has its share of manure. Sometimes it doesn't smell very good. But the way we handle life's manure makes our life-force bloom.

But the farmer is right . . . meditation is good for nothing. Meditation is not a means to get anything. Sure, there are some benefits. You can experience increased awareness, mental peace, and spiritual security. But nothing can keep you from old age, sickness, and death.

Real peace is to be one with where you are. You can spend your whole life trying to get something, meanwhile missing the moment at hand. There's a Zen saying, "If you want to attain suchness, you should practice suchness without delay." This is "meditation". If you're looking for peace and silence, you might find a little of it on a cushion. But true "peace and silence" is to be one with whatever circumstances you are in.

True meditation is to take care of what's in front of you. Plow the rows and pull the weeds! If things are not going your way, can you continue to plow the rows and deal with the weeds? This is taking care of life as it is. Farmers have to deal with many difficult circumstances. Barns burn. Tornados and droughts happen. Maintaining continuity is the life of a true farmer.

We're all called to be "monks and farmers". Everyone is required to quiet their mind and to sit up in their life. Things take their own time and have their own course. You can't always control a river.

Life requires real perseverance. It is like the flow of a stream that carves a hole in a rock. Sometimes you feel like a fool and an idiot. This is where I think the monk and the farmer have a lot in common. We're all working with the same thing. It's called life!

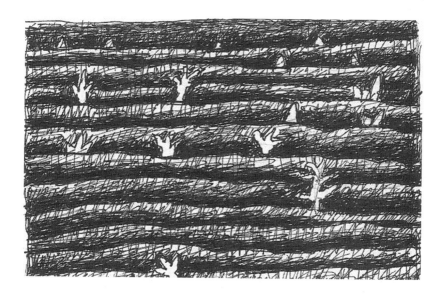

Love's Nobility

Sept. 3, 2015

A while back I was in a Wendy's restaurant having a bite to eat. I noticed an older couple sitting at a table. They seemed to be having a nice meal together. Then later, I noticed that the older gentleman had brought their car around to the front door of the Wendy's. Then I saw that he was walking backwards with his elderly wife holding on to both of his hands. She was just able to creep along and he held her steadily as she moved forward with him walking backwards. They eventually got to the car and he helped her get in to the front seat.

I was really struck with the scene. It was very intimate. It was a whole lifetime captured in a moment. I thought to myself this was love in its fullest expression.

I referred to this incident in a recent wedding where I was officiating. I offered this story as a wedding wish for the young couple. Everyone was touched by the scene. It became our communal wish for the couple.

Attraction and desire are a beautiful stage of love. But being able to walk together for the long walk is even more beautiful. This old couple has shared many walks, I'm sure. But this one that I saw was perhaps their most inimate.

The Buddha had this to say about marriage: "Oh, husband and wife! Respect and love each other by filling up what one lacks with what another has! Do not become greedy! Grudge not in giving! Be always benign in speech and manner! Sometimes minds quarrel and anger bursts forth, but any small resentment held against each other in the present may grow to be greater in life to come. The ways of mind and heart need constant guarding by love's nobility."

Love's nobility is the quality it takes to walk the long road together. The "long" road is neither long nor short. It's a matter of taking care of each moment with dignity and respect. Every moment in a person's life is a pivotal opportunity. An ancient sage said, "Form and substance are like the dew on the grass, destiny like the dart of lightning--emptied in an instant, vanished in a flash."

Time passes swiftly. It's easy to hang on to old resentments. Love's nobility requires letting go of anger and resentments. It also requires moving ahead to the moment at hand. Clearly, the old couple at Wendy's manifested love's nobility in their walk on the long road.

Acknowledgements

Thanks to **Carl Homstad** who provided the artistic dimension and designed the cover art for the book. At Carl's suggestion, the sketches for each article were contributed by local artists who are friends of Ryumonji.

Thanks to all the **Artists**! They contributed their great sketches, which add so much to this offering. The names of all the artists are listed on the next page.

Thanks to **Sheryl Myoshin Lilke** who did such a wonderful job of editing the articles for this book and offered her heartfelt encouragement.

Thank you to **Eishin Tom Houghton and Mary Myo-an McCulley** who laid the ground-work for publication.

Thanks to **Taizen Dale VerKuilen** and **Joe Kyugen Michaud** who offered their counsel on publication issues.

Appreciation to our publisher, **Clark Kenyon** of Camp Pope Publishing, who guided us through the forests of publication.

And special thanks to the **Decorah Newspapers** who for years has invited local clergy to write a column in their newspaper. They graciously gave their permission to print these articles for this collection.

And finally a special thanks to the **rivers, rocks, trees,** and **grasses** and **all the sentient beings** that are manifestations of this great Universe.

Artists for the Sketches

Zen Glossary

Buddha – Buddha in Sanskrit literally means "enlightened one". It is a reference to the historical Gotama Shakyamuni who lived in northern India in 500 B.C. "Buddha" was a common title for any teacher who had some degree of enlightenment or awareness. Gotama Shakyamuni came to be called "the Buddha".

Buddhism – One of the world religions. It is a way of living rather than a belief system. The Buddha's last words were: "Each person should be a lamp unto themselves." Many cultures tend to "divinize" the Buddha, but the Buddha never claimed any kind of divinity or divine inspiration. He reflected on the nature of life and saw the inter-dynamic relatedness of all phenomenal existence. Thus the phrase, "Form is emptiness, emptiness is form." Everything is empty of its own substantiality and full of all existence. For instance if you see a tree, you should see the earth, the sun, and rain from the heavens. This is tree as it truly is. This is also true of you and me. If you see this inter-dynamic oneness, then you should live a life of gratitude and compassion for all beings.

Dana – Dana is the Sanskrit word for free-will offerings.

Dharma – These are the teachings of the Buddha. They are accessible to everyone. They can be seen through a teacher, the sutras, or through your own practice of meditation. The teachings of the Buddha came to be spread from master to disciple through India, East Asian countries, and now to the West.

Dharma Transmission – This is a lengthy process whereby a novice monk studies with a teacher in the daily living of Zen teachings. This transmission is acknowledged in a formal personal ceremony between the teacher and monk. The monk receives the seal of recognition from the teacher that she or he is a Dharma successor. This process of direct transmission from master to disciple has existed for over 2500 years.

Dogen – Dogen was a Japanese Zen monk who traveled to China. He practiced for five years with a Chinese master named Tendo Nyojo. Dogen received Dharma Transmission from this master and successfully transmitted the Soto Zen lineage to Japan in 1227. He is considered the founder of Japanese Soto Zen.

Enlightenment – Enlightenment is not something to be attained but to be lived. It is a respectful awareness of the interpenetrated nature of all existence. It is rising to meet the causes and conditions of what transpires in one's life.

Koan – Koans are teachings from ancient times of everyday incidents between teachers and their disciples. The intent is to show the relationship between the consequences of daily life events and their impact on the future.

Mindfulness – Mindfulness is a quality of meditation. It includes being aware of self and others.

Oryoki Meals – These are the formal meals conducted during retreats and extended practice periods called "angos". Each person has a set of bowls to use during the retreat. The meal chant begins, "Innumerable labors have brought us this food. We should know how it comes to us." The chants emphasize a spirit of appreciation for food and that we eat for our own health and for the benefit of all beings. Literally, oryoki means to receive what's offered.

Rinzai Zen – Rinzai Zen is a branch of Zen Buddhism that came down to present day through a Zen monk in China named Rinzai.

Roshi – Roshi is a title of "Senior Teacher". It is used in conjunction with the name of the teacher.

Sangha – Sangha is a Sanskrit word from the Buddha's time which means Community. From earliest times people sat in meditation with other practitioners. It is helpful to self and others to sit in community.

Sesshins – Sesshins are Zen retreats with a set schedule of meditation, work, lecture and service. Sesshin literally means "collecting the mind". They can last from one day to one week.

Soto Zen – Soto Zen is a reference to the lineage of Dharma transmission that occurred through two Chinese masters. Their names were Sozan and Tozan. The reference to Soto lineage is taken from the first Chinese character of the names of these two Chinese Zen masters.

Sutras – Sutras are the recorded teachings of Buddhas and ancestors. They are the scriptures of Buddhism. These teachings were transmitted verbally for centuries and then recorded in various collections.

Takuhatsu – Takuhatsu is the practice of mendicant begging. In ancient times Buddhist monks supported themselves with the free-will offerings of local people.

Zazen – Zazen is the practice of up-right sitting meditation. It is usually conducted with folded legs sitting on a round cushion, called a "zafu". You can also sit on a chair. The right hand is placed under the left hand with thumb tips touching. Eyes are half open. The tongue is placed on the roof of the mouth with teeth and lips both shut. The basic instruction for what to do with your mind is to "think not thinking". But how do you "think not thinking?" "Non-thinking." Non-thinking is clear and unbiased mind. Just take care of the moment at hand. This is the essential art of zazen.

Zen – Zen is a reference to the basic meditation practice that was transmitted from the Buddha to the present age. In the

Soto Zen lineage it has come down through India, China and Japan. In India this practice of meditation was called "Dhyana". In China it was called "Chan". In Japan it was called "Zen". Thus Zen Buddhism refers to Buddhism that came to the West through Japanese Zen teachers. There is also Tibetan Buddhism which came from India through Tibet and Theravada Buddhism which came from India through Thailand and other East Asian countries. All of these branches of Buddhism can be found in the West today.

Zen Centers – Zen Centers are in many cities and towns across this country. You can search for them on the internet. They usually have a schedule of sitting meditation and retreats and public lectures. They are open to anyone.

Additional Copies May be Ordered through

Ryumonji Zen Monastery

2452 Ryumon Road

Dorchester, IA 52140

Email: Office@Ryumonji.Org

By phone: 563- 546-1309